# PETS UNDERCOVER!

# The TRUTH About HAMSTERS

## What Hamsters Do When You're Not Looking

MARY COLSON

raintree

a Capstone company — publishers for children

Raintree is an imprint of Capstone Global Library Limited, a company incorporated in England and Wales having its registered office at 264 Banbury Road, Oxford, OX2 7DY – Registered company number: 6695582

**www.raintree.co.uk**
myorders@raintree.co.uk

Edited by Helen Cox Cannons
Designed by Philippa Jenkins
Picture research by Morgan Walters
Production by Laura Manthe
Originated by Capstone Global Library Limited
Printed and bound in China

ISBN 978 1 4747 3851 4
21 20 19 18 17
10 9 8 7 6 5 4 3 2 1

**British Library Cataloguing in Publication Data**
A full catalogue record for this book is available from the British Library.

**Acknowledgements**
We would like to thank the following for permission to reproduce photographs: All photographs by Justin Hoffmann at Pixelfox.

We would like to thank Anastasia Blair BA (Hons) for her invaluable help in the preparation of this book.

Some words are shown in bold, **like this**. You can find out what they mean by looking in the glossary.

# CONTENTS

# Hello!

Hello! My name's Bonnie. I'm slow to like people usually but you seem pretty cool. It's best to let me do my own thing. If you do that, we'll get along fine.

I live with my owner, Tom, and his Dad. When they are out, I get up to all sorts of things! I may look cute but don't be fooled – I'm really wild!

# I don't do mornings

No! It can't be morning already! I don't like being woken up! I like my cosy nest. If I stay very still, Tom will leave me alone. He knows better than to disturb me. I much prefer night-time. Tom and I can play together then. I'm far more awake at night.

# Snack time!

I think the coast is clear now. Oh, yum! Tom's left me all my favourites. I have carrots, tomatoes, celery, sweetcorn, seeds and nuts. With my cheek **pouches**, I can carry snacks to my store. I then eat the food later.

I often have a little nibble on some **bark**. This is to keep my teeth short and sharp.

# Keeping clean

It takes a lot of **grooming** to look this good! I lick my front paws to get them wet. Then, I use them like a sponge to wash my face. I do this after eating. I don't want bits of food messing up my lovely smooth fur.

# On the move

What's going on? Ooh, great! Tom's left the cage door open! Yippee, I'm free! Tom's Dad is always telling him to close the cage door properly.

Right, where shall I go first? I love exploring! I know – I will go to my favourite **look-out post**. I like to see everything that's going on.

# Marking my patch

Ooh, there's a chair leg. I'm going to rub my **scent glands** on it. I have special glands on my hips. I put my smell onto everything, from furniture to Tom! The smell reminds me that this is my **patch**.

# Keeping fit the wild way

Aww! Tom closed the cage door last night. Sigh. Today, I'm going to run around my cage instead.

I love running on my wheel. Whee! Round and round, I go! I also like climbing over logs. When I play like this, I'm keeping fit. I need to be strong in case I ever need to defend myself and my **patch**.

# Fang-tastic!

Check out my terrific teeth!
My teeth are growing all the time.
I have to **gnaw** things to keep
them short. If they grow too long,
I won't be able to eat. Gnawing
also helps keep my teeth sharp.

I gnaw on anything, from food
to furniture. I often gnaw on my
cage bars. I shouldn't do this,
really – it squashes my nose!

# Alarm bells

Squeal! What's this? A giant hand is coming into my cage! I have poor eyesight and I don't like surprises. I get scared when things appear right in front of me. My wild nature is to attack and I might bite. On second thoughts, I'm going to hide in my bed!

# Grab and go!

Oh, that's a nice bit of cardboard. I can use that! Tom has given me some tissues as well. Brilliant! I'm a great collector. I love creating **stockpiles** of bits and pieces. I **shred** them and use them to make my nest.

# Playing around

When Tom comes home, I'm ready to play. He's very gentle with me.

Tom takes me out of my cage and lets me run on the floor. I also sit on his lap and run up his arms. He blocks up any possible escape routes, though. Tom knows I might dart off and hide while he's looking the other way!

# When you go to sleep...

Lights out for Tom means the fun really starts for me! I'm **nocturnal** so I love night-time.

Once Tom is asleep, I can make a racket! I run around, climb and burrow in my bedding. I always stay **alert** – you never know where the next danger lies. It's best to be ready.

Great! Looks like Tom forgot to shut the cage door again. I'm off!

# How wild is *your* hamster?

**1.** What might your hamster do if you wake it up?

**a)** It snuggles down deeper into its bed.

**b)** It gets up and runs around on its wheel, happy to play.

**c)** It shows its sharp teeth and looks like it might bite you!

**2.** What does your hamster do when it plays?

**a)** It stands on its back legs and looks cute.

**b)** It checks out things that you put in the cage.

**c)** It runs around and around either on its wheel, in its cage or all over you!

**3.** What does your hamster do to practise its fighting skills?

**a)** It makes quick dashes across the cage then back again.

**b)** It pretends to run against the sides of its cage.

**c)** It races around its cage, over logs and through tunnels as quickly as possible!

**4.** What does your hamster do if its cage door is left open?

**a)** It is so laid back and sleepy, it doesn't notice.

**b)** It slowly sniffs around the cage door checking for possible danger.

**c)** It doesn't wait to ask permission, it's out of there!

To find out how wild your hamster is, check the results on page 32.

# Glossary

**alert**  quick to notice something

**bark**  outside layer of a tree

**gnaw**  chew hard on something

**grooming**  keeping clean and tidy

**look-out post**  high place that gives a good view

**nocturnal**  sleepy in the day, awake at night

**patch**  territory; area where something lives or roams

**pouch**  pocket-like space

**scent glands**  special organs in the body that make smells

**shred**  rip into small pieces

**stockpile**  large supply of something

# Find out more

## Books

*Hamsters: Questions and Answers* (Pet Questions and Answers), Christina Mia Gardeski (Raintree, 2016)

*Hip Hamster Projects* (Pet Projects), Isabel Thomas (Raintree, 2015)

*Nibble's Guide to Caring for Your Hamster* (Pets' Guides), Anita Ganeri (Raintree, 2013)

## Websites

**http://www.rspca.org.uk/adviceandwelfare/ pets/rodents/hamsters**
This page on the RSPCA website is full of fascinating facts about hamsters and how to care for them.

# Index

**Quiz answers:**

**Mostly As:** Your hamster is cute and picture perfect. It is chilled out and happy to snooze the day away. It is not what you would call wild!

**Mostly Bs:** Your hamster is pretty wild. It loves to play, run and chase. It's also on the look-out for danger.

**Mostly Cs:** Your hamster is totally out of control. It's as wild as they come! Make sure you keep its cage door firmly shut!